SRA Early Interventions in Reading

Reading

Pen Pals Across the Pacific

By
Carole Gerber

Illustrated by
Oki Han

SRA

Columbus, OH

The **McGraw-Hill** Companies

Photo Credits

6 ©Yang Liu/CORBIS.

SRAonline.com

 SRA

Send all inquiries to:
SRA/McGraw-Hill
8787 Orion Place
Columbus, OH 43240-4027

Printed in the United States of America.

ISBN 0-07-604472-6

2 3 4 5 6 7 8 9 MAL 10 09 08 07 06

Contents

Chapter 1
Hello!

Dear Pen Pal,

Ni hao! My name is Li Ming, but my relatives and friends call me Mingming. *Ni hao* means "hello" in China, where I live.

I'm not sure how much you know about China. My teacher says I should tell you about it. In return, she says you might tell me endless things about the United States.

In China the government controls what people do more closely than in the United States. The government makes sure everyone has food and shelter. China is a little smaller in size than the United States, but our population is much bigger. About one billion people live in China—about four times more than the United States! I think life is very different here than it is where you live.

I've never had a pen pal. I breathlessly await your letter and would be very grateful if you wrote back!

Sincerely,

Mingming

Ni hao, Mingming!

I'm excited to hear from you and hope you can give me bottomless info about China. Why are you called Mingming instead of Li, since that name comes first? My name is Paula Franklin. I live in San Diego, California, and I have a brother named Dwight. What's the name of your city? Do you any brothers or sisters?

Your pen pal,

Paula

Dear Paula,

In China, our last name comes before our first. My dad is Li Jun, and my mom is Wong Pei—women keep their last names after marriage. It is best for our country to have small families, so I have no siblings. I live in Kowloon. Tell me how to say your city—the letters are difficult and meaningless to me. I'm hopeful you can help.

Sincerely,

Mingming

Dear Mingming,

Here's how you say the name of my city: San Dee-a-go. San Diego is on the coast where it's gorgeous most of the time.

I like our zoo. In one part, the animals roam free in limitless areas. People ride in buses to look at animals wandering around. Do you have a zoo in Kowloon?

Your pal,

Paula

Dear Paula,

In Hong Kong's zoo, the animals are in cages. It would be interesting to see them roaming freely like in your zoo! Kowloon, too, is on the sea. I am enclosing a photograph of my city for you. Kowloon means "nine dragons," but there are no dragons—just harmless shops. I made a joke!

Sincerely,

Mingming

Dear Mingming,

Thanks for the photograph of Kowloon. There seem to be an endless number of bright, colorful lights everywhere! I wish I could visit your city. How big is Kowloon? I researched San Diego's population and learned that almost three million people reside here. Wow! I had no idea there were that many.

Your pal,

Paula

P.S. I liked your joyful joke!

Dear Paula,

I didn't know Kowloon's size, so my teacher told me to look on the computer. I learned that about two million people live here. It's big but not quite as large as San Diego.

There are many small, disconnected shops. As you can see, most shops have neon signs that flash ceaselessly and look really magnificent at night.

I've heard there are many cars in San Diego. Here there are not so many. Most people walk or ride bicycles. There's lots of sometimes reckless traffic—my teacher says Americans say "hustle and bustle." Kowloon is across Victoria Harbor from Hong Kong, where there are many successful banks. Kowloon has the shops. I love shopping. Do you?

Sincerely,

Mingming

Chapter 2
What Is Your Family Like?

Dear Mingming,

I like to shop too! I especially like shopping for clothes and toys, but I don't get to shop for them often. However, every week I go food shopping with my dad. We go to a big grocery store, and he always lets me push the cart. I get to choose my favorite healthful cereal.

Sometimes the people who work at the grocery store give free samples. Last week we tasted ice cream. Yum! Dad bought some to bring home. We also tried some cheese, but I disliked it. It was pretty tasteless.

I told Dad about all the bicycle riders in China. He said it would be good exercise instead of driving everywhere.

Your pal,

Paula

Dear Paula,

We buy food at shops in Mong Kok market. My grandmother and I buy chicken at one shop and then go to another for vegetables and fruits. We shop at bigger stores for clothes and toys.

My grandmother rides a bicycle. I love her very much, and I am very thankful for her. Does your grandmother live near you? What's your family like?

Sincerely,

Mingming

Dear Mingming,

Shopping with your grandmother sounds pleasant. It's so cool that she rides a bike! She sounds fearless! I'm not sure my grandmother knows how. I'll ask her when I see her. She lives far away.

I have to set the table for dinner, so good-bye for now. What do you look like? Please send a picture!

Your pal,

Paula

Dear Paula,

I asked my teacher what kind of picture you wanted me to send, and she said to send a photograph. That's what I have enclosed. My teacher said I should also tell you about my parents and their careers and other helpful facts. My father works for a hotel in Kowloon. My mother teaches at a nursery school.

My grandmother moved from the countryside to live with us after my grandfather died. She's been here since I was a baby and seems ageless. She walks with me to school, watches me while my parents work, and cooks dinner for us every night.

Please send a photograph and facts about your family.

Sincerely,

Mingming

Dear Mingming,

You look so pretty! Your parents and your grandmother look very friendly and delightful. I'm taking the picture to school to show my class.

We're having a family photograph taken soon. I'll send you one of those so you can see what we look like. I promise to write you more later!

Your pal,

Paula

Dear Mingming,

I'm writing again to tell you about my family. My dad's name is Jeremiah. He's a salesman. I think he's in his thirties. So is my mom. Her name is Anita, and she works part-time in a bookstore. My brother Dwight is six. Sometimes he's brainless but also funny. I'll send our picture soon!

Your pal,

Paula

Dear Paula,

Thank you for the wonderful two letters—they arrived yesterday. My parents are both thirty-six, and my grandmother is seventy-two.

It's nice that your mother works in a bookstore. My teacher says about 90 percent of China's people can read and write. She says literacy is important to our people.

Could you please describe your school?

Sincerely,

Mingming

Chapter 3
Do You Enjoy School?

Dear Mingming,

We finally had our family picture taken, and I'm sending one along with this letter.

My brother and I go to Tristan Elementary School. We really like the school. My dad says it's an excellent school that will prepare us for the future. Mom says my brother and I are very lucky to go there.

Do you like school?

Your pal,

Paula

Dear Paula,

Thank you for the photograph! Your family is extremely attractive. I like your brown eyes. Mine are brown as well. I predict that we will both grow up to be very beautiful.

I attend Li Cheng Uk Government Primary School. In China, students go to school six days each week. Sometimes it seems unfair and pointless to have to go to school so much. Do you go six days a week?

Sincerely,

Mingming

Dear Mingming,

You go to school six days a week? Wow! That's unbelievable. In the United States, we go only five days—Monday through Friday. It's pretty painless. We're in school six or seven hours a day. In elementary school, we have one main classroom teacher, but we also have teachers for music, art, and gym. I prefer math and dislike art. What's school like in China?

Your pal,

Paula

Dear Paula,

School is quite difficult in China. All students have six years of primary school. Then everyone takes exams to test their previous knowledge. Only about one-third pass and go on to secondary school. Students in big cities like mine have more courses and study the English language. Many villages have only primary schools. Grandmother says I'm lucky to live in Kowloon.

Grandmother went only to primary school in her village.

I work hard in school and expect to pass the tests I've prepared for, and then I'll go to secondary school for six years. My father says only 2 percent of students go to university. My parents expect me to go.

Science is my favorite subject.

Sincerely,

Mingming

Dear Mingming,

I read your letter to my parents. They say everyone here is offered twelve years of free school. Some people find jobs, but many students go on to college. The government tries to help everyone find the money to go to college, regardless of who they are, to make sure no one is prevented from going.

What do you do for fun?

Your pal,

Paula

Dear Paula,

Like many people in China, my parents and I like to fly kites. I learned in school that kites were invented about 2,500 years ago by Chinese people.

The frames that make the shapes of our kites are premade with bamboo, which is an almost weightless hollow wood. Then the bamboo is covered with silk cloth to form the kite.

I don't boast when I say that Chinese kites are the most beautiful in the world. I have several kites, and each is different. All are hand painted. My favorite is a butterfly. When families fly kites in the park, the sky is filled with displays of stunning silk creatures. I like to pretend they're alive!

Please write about what you and your family do.

Sincerely,

Mingming

Dear Mingming,

I love hearing about Chinese kites. It's so captivating! I hope you don't mind that I discussed your letter with my class. Everyone has asked if you'd send a photograph of one of your kites.

My family likes to surf. I'll tell you more about it next time. Right now I have to preheat a snack. I can't wait to see your kite!

Your pal,

Paula

Chapter 4
What Do You Do for Fun?

Dear Paula,

I'm delighted your class found the facts about Chinese kites to be so enthralling. I enclose a photograph of my favorite kite. It's 102 centimeters by 115 centimeters in size.

What does it mean to "surf"? That word is meaningless to me, and my teacher doesn't know what it means either. Tell me all about it, please.

Sincerely,

Mingming

Dear Mingming,

Your kite is awesome! My teacher says it's so beautiful that it should be hanging in a museum. It doesn't look tattered by the wind.

To surf, I stand on a special kind of board and "ride" ocean waves. I have to take precautions to stay safe, but still sometimes I lose my balance. It's fun to tumble into the water!

Your pal,

Paula

Dear Paula,

I don't think Chinese people surf, because I couldn't discover a word for "surf." My teacher said to explain to you that instead of words, we use special symbols called characters. Each character is like a picture. Each word has its own set of characters. There are thousands of characters, but I couldn't find one for "surf."

Here are the characters for "China":

Sincerely,

Mingming

P.S. Do you like music?

Dear Mingming,

I'm learning so much from you! Everyone in my class drew the characters for "China." Your way of writing is extremely different from ours!

Yes, I like music. I prefer playing an instrument called the viola that is similar to a violin but bigger. Do you play an instrument? If so, what kind?

Your pal,

Paula

Dear Paula,

Yes, I do play a musical instrument. It's like your viola because it's similar to a violin, but it's called an *erhu* and has only two strings. I know what a viola looks like. Can you imagine what an *erhu* looks like? Maybe you have seen one before. Musicians play *erhus* at our opera performances.

Sincerely,

Mingming

Dear Mingming,

No, I have never seen an *erhu,* but I went to the opera once. My teacher says opera is very popular in China because many of the stories tell about Chinese history.

I have a history question. Can you tell me about the Great Wall? I heard that astronauts can see it from space!

Your pal,

Paula

Dear Paula,

People here aren't sure if the Great Wall of China can be viewed from space. The Great Wall is about 6,700 kilometers long. That's approximately 4,200 miles, which is longer than the number of miles between the West and East coasts of the United States! People began building the wall more than two thousand years ago, and it took hundreds of years to complete. The Great Wall was built to prevent outsiders from entering China.

Sincerely,

Mingming

Dear Mingming,

Your letters are really interesting! I love learning about your culture and your life and how alike we really are.

You must practice your *erhu* a lot. I bet you play it effortlessly! I'm sure I'll never be asked to play the viola for an opera. I practice for only about fifteen minutes before dinner every night.

Speaking of food, what do people eat in 中国?

Your pal,

Paula

Dear Paula,

I'm honored to share facts with you about food in my country. Our main food is rice. In our southern regions, people eat rice for every meal. In villages everywhere, rice is all some people eat. In my family, though, we're fortunate to eat many types of food, including fish and vegetables. What foods do you like or dislike?

Sincerely,

Mingming

Chapter 5
Favorite Foods

Dear Paula,

I'm sending a second letter because my teacher said to tell you that our foods here have mostly five flavors: pungent, sour, sweet, bitter, and salty.

My family prefers small amounts of many foods. This is called dim sum. I think some restaurants in your country serve dim sum. Have you eaten this? I think it's very tasty.

Sincerely,

Mingming

Dear Mingming,

My family *loves* Chinese food and dim sum! When we order dim sum, the waiter brings a cart with a lot of choices. It's fun! My favorite is steamed dumplings with pork and shrimp. I can't remember the words for these. Can you remind me?

Your pal,

Paula

P.S. Here's a picture I drew of my favorite food!

Dear Paula,

The name for those dumplings is *sui mai*. I also like *sui mai*. Someday you should taste the cake made with turnips, called *lo bak go.*

Your hamburger picture looks delicious. I've eaten hamburgers at fast-food restaurants here, but my grandmother thinks fast food is tasteless. My father says some American guests at the hotel ask where to find fast food.

Sincerely,

Mingming

Dear Mingming,

My family prepares and eats most of our meals at home. When we have hamburgers, my dad usually grills them outdoors.

I told my parents about the cake you recommended. Mom says next time we order dim sum, we'll choose *lo bak go* for dessert!

What kinds of fast-food restaurants are in China?

Your pal,

Paula

Dear Paula,

We have all kinds of fast food. There are American fast-food restaurants that sell hamburgers and pizza, but there's also other fast food. Our fast food includes things like noodles, dumplings, and steamed bread. I disagree with my grandmother: I like to eat all kinds of fast food!

My family, like yours, usually eats meals at home.

Sincerely,

Mingming

Dear Mingming,

My teacher wants me to discuss how rice is grown and harvested in China. She says rice is a crop that grows in paddies. What are paddies? I told her you probably haven't harvested rice, but you said your grandmother lived in a village. Does she know how rice grows?

Write soon!

Your pal,

Paula

Dear Paula,

My grandmother lived in a village in south China, where endless amounts of rice are grown. She says my people have grown rice for more than five thousand years. She says rice is actually a kind of grass—I didn't know this! Rice is planted in paddies, which are shallow puddles. The paddies are drained before the rice is harvested.

Rice seedlings are planted one at a time by hand, spaced a hand span apart. (A span is the distance from thumb to little finger when the fingers are spread.)

Writing you has been so much fun, Paula! If you want, please continue to write to me. Who knows—maybe one day we can meet!

Sincerely,

Mingming